INSTANT DOG FOOD COOKBOOK

DR. WESLEY GLASGOW

DISCLAIMER

The content within this book reflects my thoughts, experiences, and beliefs. It is meant for informational and entertainment purposes. While I have taken great care to provide accurate information, I cannot guarantee the absolute correctness or applicability of the content to every individual or situation. Please consult with relevant professionals for advice specific to your needs.

TABLE OF CONTENTS

INTRODUCTION

In the quiet corners of my childhood, amidst laughter and fleeting summers, my love for dogs was born. Growing up, my world revolved around the pitter-patter of paws and the unwavering loyalty of my four-legged companions. It was a bond that transcended words, a connection that fuelled my journey from a passionate dog lover to a devoted advocate for their well-being.

My parents, recognizing the depth of my affection for our canine friends, presented me with a gift that would forever shape the trajectory of my life – a furry bundle of joy named Dan. From the very first moment our eyes met, a profound understanding blossomed. Dan became more than a pet; he was family, a confidant in my growing years, a silent companion through the highs and lows of adolescence.

In the innocence of youth, I expressed my love through abundance. Dan was my joy, and I showered him with treats, indulging his every whim. We shared countless moments of joy and companionship, his tail wagging in blissful response to my every gesture. However, as time marched forward, an invisible storm gathered on the horizon, threatening the tranquility of our cherished bond.

After a few short years of bliss, Dan's health took an unexpected turn. The exuberance that once defined him was replaced by lethargy, and his once agile frame bore the weight of an unseen burden. A trip to the veterinarian revealed a harsh truth – Dan was diagnosed with diabetes, a cruel blow to our unbreakable connection. His diet, once filled with the exuberance of youth, needed a radical transformation.

The realization struck me with the force of a thunderclap – the power of good nutrition to shape the destiny of those we love. Witnessing the transformation in Dan's health through a carefully curated diet ignited a passion within me. That defining moment marked the genesis of my unwavering commitment to the well-being of dogs, a commitment that led me down a path of knowledge, exploration, and advocacy.

Today, after 25 years of tireless dedication to understanding the intricate tapestry of canine nutrition, I stand before you not just as a seasoned veterinarian but as a culinary guide for your beloved pets. My name is Dr. Wesley Glasgow, and I welcome you to a world where love is expressed through nourishment, where each meal is a testament to the unspoken bond between humans and their faithful companions.

As I weave together this Instant Pot Dog Food Cookbook, I am driven by the questions that echo through the corridors of every dog lover's heart: How can we provide our furry friends with meals that speak to their vitality, that resonate with the echoes of ancestral diets, and that echo the joy they bring into our lives?

Within these pages, we explore the profound benefits of healthy eating for dogs – the boundless energy, the lustrous coat, the sparkle in their eyes – a symphony of well-being orchestrated through the culinary choices we make for our pets. Equally, we delve into the dangers of unhealthy eating, unearthing the consequences that lurk in the shadows, threatening to cast a pall over the lives of those who bring us immeasurable joy.

This cookbook is not just a collection of recipes; it is a testament to the transformative power of mindful nutrition. Within its embrace, you will discover a culinary journey that transcends the ordinary, crafting meals that resonate with the heartbeats of your faithful companions. The advantage of this cookbook lies not just in its recipes but in the promise it holds – the promise of a healthier, happier life for your beloved pets.

Join me on this odyssey, where pots simmer with love, and the aroma of wholesome ingredients fills the air. Let us embark on a journey that transcends the boundaries of ordinary cookbooks, a journey that celebrates the timeless bond between humans and their cherished dogs. Welcome to a world where every meal is an expression of love, a symphony of health, and a promise of joy.

Contact the Author

Thank you for reading my book! I would love to hear from you, whether you have feedback, questions, or just want to share your thoughts. Your feedback means a lot to me and helps me improve as a writer.

Please don't hesitate to reach out to me through

glasgowesley@gmail.com

I look forward to connecting with my readers and appreciate your support in this literary journey. Your thoughts and comments are valuable to me.

CHAPTER 1

Understanding Dog Nutrition

Dogs, like humans, require a balanced and nutritious diet to thrive. Providing the right nutrients in the correct proportions is crucial for their overall health and well-being. Here's a breakdown of essential aspects of dog nutrition, including essential nutrients, portion control, feeding guidelines, and common allergens.

Essential Nutrients for Dogs:

1. **Proteins:** Essential for muscle development, repair, and overall body function. Sources include meat, poultry, fish, and plant-based proteins.

2. **Fats:** Important for energy, skin health, and a shiny coat. Sources include animal fats, fish oil, and plant-based oils.

3. **Carbohydrates:** Provide a source of energy. Common sources include grains, vegetables, and legumes.

4. **Vitamins:** Essential for various metabolic processes. Dogs need a range of vitamins, including A, B, C, D, and E. These can be obtained from a balanced diet.

5. **Minerals:** Important for bone health, enzyme function, and overall well-being. Key minerals include calcium, phosphorus, potassium, and zinc.

6. **Water:** Vital for hydration and overall bodily functions. Always ensure your dog has access to clean and fresh water.

Portion Control and Feeding Guidelines:

1. **Caloric Needs:** The appropriate portion size depends on factors such as the dog's size, age, activity level, and health condition. Consult your veterinarian to determine the right calorie intake for your dog.

2. **Scheduled Meals:** Establish a regular feeding schedule, typically two meals per day for adult dogs. Puppies may require more frequent meals.

3. **Avoid Overfeeding:** Obesity is a common issue in dogs. Measure portions and avoid feeding table scraps to maintain a healthy weight.

4. **Special Diets:** Some dogs may require special diets due to medical conditions. Consult your vet if you suspect your dog has specific nutritional needs.

Common Dog Food Allergens:

1. **Grains:** Wheat, soy, and corn are common allergens. Consider grain-free options if your dog exhibits sensitivity.

2. **Proteins:** Some dogs may be allergic to specific protein sources like beef, chicken, or fish.

3. **Dairy:** Lactose intolerance can be common, so monitor for signs of digestive issues after consuming dairy products.

4. **Artificial Additives:** Colorings, preservatives, and flavorings can trigger allergies in some dogs. Opt for natural and high-quality dog food.

CHAPTER 2

Getting Started with the Instant Pot

The Instant Pot has become a popular kitchen appliance known for its versatility and efficiency. It's a multi-functional electric pressure cooker that can also be used as a slow cooker, rice cooker, steamer, sauté pan, and more. Understanding its features and functions can help you make the most of this convenient kitchen tool.

1. **Pressure Cooking:** The Instant Pot uses pressure to cook food quickly, making it an excellent time-saving device.

2. **Settings:** Instant Pots typically come with various settings for different cooking methods, such as sautéing, slow cooking, and yogurt making.

3. **Safety Features:** Built-in safety features, including pressure release valves and locking mechanisms, ensure safe operation.

4. **Size Options:** Instant Pots come in various sizes, catering to different household needs. Common sizes include 3, 6, and 8 quarts.

Tips for Cooking Dog Food in the Instant Pot:

Making dog food in the Instant Pot can be a convenient and nutritious option. Here are some tips to get you started:

1. **Balanced Diet:** Ensure your dog's food includes a mix of proteins, fats, and carbohydrates. Consult with your veterinarian to create a well-balanced recipe.

2. **Protein Sources:** Use lean meats like chicken, turkey, or beef as the primary protein source. Remove bones and excess fat before cooking.

3. **Vegetables and Grains:** Add dog-friendly vegetables like carrots, peas, and sweet potatoes. Include grains like rice or quinoa for additional nutrients.

4. **Avoid Seasonings:** Keep the dog food simple and free from added seasonings, salt, and spices. Dogs have different taste preferences, and they may not tolerate certain seasonings well.

5. **Cooking Time:** Adjust cooking times based on the ingredients used. Meat and vegetables usually require less cooking time compared to grains.

Safety Considerations:

1. **Read the Manual:** Familiarize yourself with the Instant Pot's user manual to understand its features and safety guidelines.

2. **Proper Sealing:** Always ensure the Instant Pot is properly sealed before cooking under pressure. Follow the instructions for sealing and venting.

3. **Release Pressure Safely:** When the cooking cycle is complete, release pressure according to the recipe instructions. Be cautious of hot steam and follow the recommended release method.

4. **Avoid Overfilling:** Do not overfill the Instant Pot to prevent potential safety hazards. Follow the recommended maximum fill lines for liquids and solids.

5. **Regular Maintenance:** Keep the Instant Pot clean and well-maintained. Regularly check the sealing ring, steam release valve, and other components for wear and tear.

CHAPTER 3
Wholesome Grain and Veggie Mixes

Chicken and Rice Delight:

Cooking Time: 22 minutes (12 minutes cooking + 10 minutes natural release)

Servings: 4

Ingredients:

- 1 cup boneless, skinless chicken breast, diced
- 1 cup brown rice
- 1 cup sweet potatoes, diced
- 1/2 cup carrots, chopped
- 4 cups low-sodium chicken broth

Instructions:

1. Place diced chicken, brown rice, sweet potatoes, carrots, and chicken broth into the Instant Pot.

2. Secure the lid, set the Instant Pot to Manual mode at high pressure, and cook for 12 minutes.

3. Once the cooking cycle is complete, allow for a natural release for 10 minutes.

4. After the natural release, carefully perform a quick release to release any remaining pressure.

5. Open the lid, stir the mixture well, and let it cool before serving to your dog.

Nutritional Information: Per serving - Calories: 320, Protein: 22g, Fat: 5g, Carbohydrates: 45g

Turkey and Quinoa Bliss:

Cooking Time: 15 minutes (10 minutes cooking + quick release)

Servings: 3

Ingredients:

- 1 cup ground turkey

- 1 cup quinoa, rinsed

- 1 cup green beans, chopped

- 1/2 cup pumpkin puree

- 3 cups low-sodium vegetable broth

Instructions:

1. Select the sauté mode on the Instant Pot and brown the ground turkey.

2. Add in the rinsed quinoa, chopped green beans, pumpkin puree, and low-sodium vegetable broth.

3. Switch the Instant Pot to Manual mode, set it to high pressure, and cook for 10 minutes.

4. Once the cooking time is complete, perform a quick release of pressure.

5. Stir the mixture well, and allow it to cool before serving to your dog.

Nutritional Information: Per serving - Calories: 280, Protein: 18g, Fat: 8g, Carbohydrates: 35g

Salmon and Sweet Potato Medley:

Cooking Time: 13 minutes (8 minutes cooking + 5 minutes natural release)

Servings: 2

Ingredients:

- 1 cup canned salmon, drained

- 1 cup sweet potatoes, peeled and diced

- 1/2 cup peas

- 1/2 cup brown rice

- 2 cups water

Instructions:

1. Combine canned salmon, diced sweet potatoes, peas, brown rice, and water in the Instant Pot.

2. Set the Instant Pot to Manual mode, choose high pressure, and cook for 8 minutes.

3. Allow for a natural release for 5 minutes, followed by a quick release.

4. Open the lid, fluff the rice, mix the ingredients well, and let it cool before serving.

Nutritional Information: Per serving - Calories: 250, Protein: 15g, Fat: 6g, Carbohydrates: 30g

Beef and Barley Hearty Stew:

Cooking Time: 30 minutes (20 minutes cooking + 10 minutes natural release)

Servings: 6

Ingredients:

- 1 pound lean ground beef
- 1 cup barley
- 1 cup carrots, sliced
- 1 cup green peas
- 1 can (14 oz) low-sodium beef broth

Instructions:

1. Brown the ground beef using the sauté function in the Instant Pot.
2. Add barley, carrots, green peas, and beef broth to the pot.
3. Set the Instant Pot to Manual mode, high pressure, and cook for 20 minutes.
4. Allow a natural release for 10 minutes, then perform a quick release.
5. Stir the stew, ensuring an even mix of ingredients, and let it cool before serving.

Nutritional Information: Per serving - Calories: 340, Protein: 25g, Fat: 12g, Carbohydrates: 35g

Lamb and Lentil Power Bowl:

Cooking Time: 25 minutes (15 minutes cooking + 10 minutes natural release)

Servings: 5

Ingredients:

- 1 cup ground lamb

- 1 cup lentils, rinsed

- 1 cup butternut squash, diced

- 1/2 cup spinach, chopped

- 3 cups low-sodium lamb broth

Instructions:

1. Sauté ground lamb until browned in the Instant Pot.

2. Add rinsed lentils, diced butternut squash, chopped spinach, and lamb broth.

3. Set to Manual mode, high pressure, and cook for 15 minutes.

4. Allow a natural release for 10 minutes, followed by a quick release.

5. Mix the ingredients thoroughly, and let it cool before serving.

Nutritional Information: Per serving - Calories: 290, Protein: 20g, Fat: 10g, Carbohydrates: 30g

Tuna and Quinoa Fiesta:

Cooking Time: 18 minutes (12 minutes cooking + 6 minutes natural release)

Servings: 4

Ingredients:

- 2 cans (5 oz each) tuna in water, drained

- 1 cup quinoa, rinsed

- 1 cup zucchini, diced

- 1/2 cup carrots, shredded

- 2 1/2 cups water

Instructions:

1. Combine drained tuna, rinsed quinoa, diced zucchini, shredded carrots, and water in the Instant Pot.

2. Set to Manual mode, high pressure, and cook for 12 minutes.

3. Allow a natural release for 6 minutes, followed by a quick release.

4. Fluff the quinoa and tuna mixture, and let it cool before serving.

Nutritional Information: Per serving - Calories: 220, Protein: 15g, Fat: 5g, Carbohydrates: 30g

Veggie-Packed Turkey Delight:

Cooking Time: 25 minutes (15 minutes cooking + 10 minutes natural release)

Servings: 4

Ingredients:

- 1 pound ground turkey

- 1 cup brown rice

- 1 cup broccoli, chopped

- 1/2 cup carrots, sliced

- 3 cups low-sodium turkey broth

Instructions:

1. Brown ground turkey using the sauté function in the Instant Pot.

2. Add brown rice, chopped broccoli, sliced carrots, and turkey broth.

3. Set to Manual mode, high pressure, and cook for 15 minutes.

4. Allow a natural release for 10 minutes, then perform a quick release.

5. Stir the mixture well, ensuring even distribution of ingredients, and let it cool before serving.

Nutritional Information: Per serving - Calories: 300, Protein: 20g, Fat: 8g, Carbohydrates: 35g

Pork and Potato Harvest Stew:

Cooking Time: 28 minutes (18 minutes cooking + 10 minutes natural release)

Servings: 5

Ingredients:

- 1 cup lean pork, diced

- 1 cup potatoes, peeled and cubed

- 1 cup green beans, cut into small pieces

- 1/2 cup apples, diced

- 2 cups low-sodium pork broth

Instructions:

1. Sauté diced pork until browned using the Instant Pot's sauté function.

2. Add potatoes, green beans, diced apples, and pork broth.

3. Set to Manual mode, high pressure, and cook for 18 minutes.

4. Allow a natural release for 10 minutes, then quick release.

5. Gently stir the stew, ensuring all ingredients are well combined, and let it cool before serving.

Nutritional Information: Per serving - Calories: 260, Protein: 18g, Fat: 7g, Carbohydrates: 30g

Chicken and Pumpkin Power Pot:

Cooking Time: 20 minutes (15 minutes cooking + 5 minutes natural release)

Servings: 3

Ingredients:

- 1 cup chicken thighs, boneless and skinless, diced

- 1 cup pumpkin, peeled and diced

- 1/2 cup peas

- 1 cup brown rice

- 2 1/2 cups low-sodium chicken broth

Instructions:

1. Combine diced chicken thighs, diced pumpkin, peas, brown rice, and chicken broth in the Instant Pot.

2. Set to Manual mode, high pressure, and cook for 15 minutes.

3. Allow a natural release for 5 minutes, then perform a quick release.

4. Stir the mixture gently, ensuring all ingredients are evenly distributed, and let it cool before serving.

Nutritional Information: Per serving - Calories: 290, Protein: 16g, Fat: 6g, Carbohydrates: 35g

Veggie-Filled Lamb and Rice Mix:

Cooking Time: 22 minutes (12 minutes cooking + 10 minutes natural release)

Servings: 4

Ingredients:

- 1 cup ground lamb
- 1 cup brown rice
- 1 cup carrots, sliced
- 1/2 cup green peas
- 3 cups low-sodium lamb broth

Instructions:

1. Brown ground lamb using the sauté function in the Instant Pot.
2. Add brown rice, sliced carrots, green peas, and lamb broth.
3. Set to Manual mode, high pressure, and cook for 12 minutes.
4. Allow a natural release for 10 minutes, then quick release.
5. Stir the mixture thoroughly, ensuring a well-mixed texture, and let it cool before serving.

Nutritional Information: Per serving - Calories: 330, Protein: 22g, Fat: 9g, Carbohydrates: 40g

CHAPTER 4
Pawsitively Delicious Stews

Chicken and Sweet Potato Harmony:

Cooking Time: 25 minutes (15 minutes cooking + 10 minutes natural release)

Servings: 4

Ingredients:

- 1 pound boneless, skinless chicken thighs, diced

- 1 cup sweet potatoes, peeled and cubed

- 1/2 cup peas

- 1/2 cup carrots, sliced

- 3 cups low-sodium chicken broth

Instructions:

1. Add diced chicken, sweet potatoes, peas, carrots, and chicken broth to the Instant Pot.

2. Set to Manual mode, high pressure, and cook for 15 minutes.

3. Allow a natural release for 10 minutes, then perform a quick release.

4. Stir the stew thoroughly and let it cool before serving.

Nutritional Information: Per serving - Calories: 280, Protein: 18g, Fat: 6g, Carbohydrates: 30g

Beef and Pumpkin Pleasure:

Cooking Time: 28 minutes (18 minutes cooking + 10 minutes natural release)

Servings: 5

Ingredients:

- 1 pound lean beef stew meat, diced

- 1 cup pumpkin, diced

- 1 cup green beans, cut into small pieces

- 1/2 cup brown rice

- 2 cups low-sodium beef broth

Instructions:

1. Sauté diced beef in the Instant Pot until browned.

2. Add diced pumpkin, green beans, brown rice, and beef broth.

3. Set to Manual mode, high pressure, and cook for 18 minutes.

4. Allow a natural release for 10 minutes, then perform a quick release.

5. Stir the stew thoroughly and let it cool before serving.

Nutritional Information: Per serving - Calories: 320, Protein: 20g, Fat: 8g, Carbohydrates: 35g

Turkey and Quinoa Delight:

Cooking Time: 22 minutes (12 minutes cooking + 10 minutes natural release)

Servings: 4

Ingredients:

- 1 pound ground turkey

- 1 cup quinoa, rinsed

- 1 cup carrots, chopped

- 1/2 cup spinach, chopped

- 3 cups low-sodium turkey broth

Instructions:

1. Brown ground turkey in the Instant Pot.

2. Add rinsed quinoa, chopped carrots, chopped spinach, and turkey broth.

3. Set to Manual mode, high pressure, and cook for 12 minutes.

4. Allow a natural release for 10 minutes, then perform a quick release.

5. Stir the stew thoroughly and let it cool before serving.

Nutritional Information: Per serving - Calories: 290, Protein: 18g, Fat: 7g, Carbohydrates: 30g

Salmon and Lentil Bliss:

Cooking Time: 25 minutes (15 minutes cooking + 10 minutes natural release)

Servings: 4

Ingredients:

- 1 cup canned salmon, drained

- 1 cup lentils, rinsed

- 1 cup sweet potatoes, diced

- 1/2 cup green peas

- 3 cups low-sodium fish broth

Instructions:

1. Combine drained salmon, rinsed lentils, diced sweet potatoes, green peas, and fish broth in the Instant Pot.

2. Set to Manual mode, high pressure, and cook for 15 minutes.

3. Allow a natural release for 10 minutes, then perform a quick release.

4. Stir the stew thoroughly and let it cool before serving.

Nutritional Information: Per serving - Calories: 250, Protein: 16g, Fat: 6g, Carbohydrates: 30g

Pork and Apple Medley:

Cooking Time: 30 minutes (20 minutes cooking + 10 minutes natural release)

Servings: 6

Ingredients:

- 1 pound lean pork loin, diced

- 1 cup apples, peeled and chopped

- 1 cup sweet potatoes, peeled and cubed

- 1/2 cup green beans, cut into small pieces

- 4 cups low-sodium pork broth

Instructions:

1. Sauté diced pork loin until browned in the Instant Pot.

2. Add chopped apples, cubed sweet potatoes, cut green beans, and pork broth.

3. Set to Manual mode, high pressure, and cook for 20 minutes.

4. Allow a natural release for 10 minutes, then perform a quick release.

5. Stir the medley thoroughly and let it cool before serving.

Nutritional Information: Per serving - Calories: 290, Protein: 18g, Fat: 8g, Carbohydrates: 35g

Lamb and Barley Bounty:

Cooking Time: 28 minutes (18 minutes cooking + 10 minutes natural release)

Servings: 5

Ingredients:

- 1 cup ground lamb
- 1 cup barley
- 1 cup carrots, sliced
- 1/2 cup green beans, chopped
- 3 cups low-sodium lamb broth

Instructions:

1. Brown ground lamb in the Instant Pot.
2. Add barley, sliced carrots, chopped green beans, and lamb broth.
3. Set to Manual mode, high pressure, and cook for 18 minutes.
4. Allow a natural release for 10 minutes, then perform a quick release.
5. Stir the stew thoroughly and let it cool before serving.

Nutritional Information: Per serving - Calories: 330, Protein: 22g, Fat: 9g, Carbohydrates: 40g

Tuna and Brown Rice Fiesta:

Cooking Time: 20 minutes (15 minutes cooking + 5 minutes natural release)

Servings: 3

Ingredients:

- 2 cans (5 oz each) tuna in water, drained

- 1 cup brown rice

- 1 cup carrots, shredded

- 1/2 cup peas

- 2 1/2 cups water

Instructions:

1. Combine drained tuna, brown rice, shredded carrots, peas, and water in the Instant Pot.

2. Set to Manual mode, high pressure, and cook for 15 minutes.

3. Allow a natural release for 5 minutes, then perform a quick release.

4. Stir the fiesta thoroughly and let it cool before serving.

Nutritional Information: Per serving - Calories: 250, Protein: 15g, Fat: 6g, Carbohydrates: 30g

Turkey and Potato Power Pot:

Cooking Time: 22 minutes (12 minutes cooking + 10 minutes natural release)

Servings: 4

Ingredients:

- 1 pound ground turkey

- 1 cup potatoes, peeled and diced

- 1 cup green beans, cut into small pieces

- 1/2 cup pumpkin puree

- 3 cups low-sodium turkey broth

Instructions:

1. Brown ground turkey in the Instant Pot.

2. Add diced potatoes, cut green beans, pumpkin puree, and turkey broth.

3. Set to Manual mode, high pressure, and cook for 12 minutes.

4. Allow a natural release for 10 minutes, then perform a quick release.

5. Stir the power pot thoroughly and let it cool before serving.

Nutritional Information: Per serving - Calories: 300, Protein: 20g, Fat: 8g, Carbohydrates: 35g

Chicken and Barley Bliss:

Cooking Time: 25 minutes (15 minutes cooking + 10 minutes natural release)

Servings: 4

Ingredients:

- 1 pound boneless, skinless chicken breasts, diced

- 1 cup barley

- 1 cup carrots, chopped

- 1/2 cup peas

- 3 cups low-sodium chicken broth

Instructions:

1. Add diced chicken, barley, chopped carrots, peas, and chicken broth to the Instant Pot.

2. Set to Manual mode, high pressure, and cook for 15 minutes.

3. Allow a natural release for 10 minutes, then perform a quick release.

4. Stir the bliss thoroughly and let it cool before serving.

Nutritional Information: Per serving - Calories: 280, Protein: 18g, Fat: 6g, Carbohydrates: 30g

Beef and Vegetable Medley:

Cooking Time: 30 minutes (20 minutes cooking + 10 minutes natural release)

Servings: 6

Ingredients:

- 1 pound lean beef stew meat, diced

- 1 cup broccoli, chopped

- 1 cup carrots, sliced

- 1 cup brown rice

- 4 cups low-sodium beef broth

Instructions:

1. Sauté diced beef in the Instant Pot until browned.

2. Add chopped broccoli, sliced carrots, brown rice, and beef broth.

3. Set to Manual mode, high pressure, and cook for 20 minutes.

4. Allow a natural release for 10 minutes, then perform a quick release.

5. Stir the medley thoroughly and let it cool before serving.

Nutritional Information: Per serving - Calories: 310, Protein: 22g, Fat: 8g, Carbohydrates: 35g

CHAPTER 5
Meaty Delights

Beef and Quinoa Feast:

Cooking Time: 25 minutes (15 minutes cooking + 10 minutes natural release)

Servings: 4

Ingredients:

- 1 pound lean ground beef

- 1 cup quinoa, rinsed

- 1 cup sweet potatoes, diced

- 1/2 cup peas

- 3 cups low-sodium beef broth

Instructions:

1. Brown ground beef in the Instant Pot.

2. Add rinsed quinoa, diced sweet potatoes, peas, and beef broth.

3. Set to Manual mode, high pressure, and cook for 15 minutes.

4. Allow a natural release for 10 minutes, then perform a quick release.

5. Stir the feast thoroughly and let it cool before serving.

Nutritional Information: Per serving - Calories: 320, Protein: 20g, Fat: 8g, Carbohydrates: 35g

Turkey and Brown Rice Delight:

Cooking Time: 28 minutes (18 minutes cooking + 10 minutes natural release)

Servings: 5

Ingredients:

- 1 pound ground turkey

- 1 cup brown rice

- 1 cup carrots, chopped

- 1/2 cup green beans, cut into small pieces

- 3 cups low-sodium turkey broth

Instructions:

1. Brown ground turkey in the Instant Pot.

2. Add brown rice, chopped carrots, cut green beans, and turkey broth.

3. Set to Manual mode, high pressure, and cook for 18 minutes.

4. Allow a natural release for 10 minutes, then perform a quick release.

5. Stir the delight thoroughly and let it cool before serving.

Nutritional Information: Per serving - Calories: 300, Protein: 18g, Fat: 7g, Carbohydrates: 30g

Chicken and Barley Banquet:

Cooking Time: 22 minutes (12 minutes cooking + 10 minutes natural release)

Servings: 4

Ingredients:

- 1 pound boneless, skinless chicken thighs, diced

- 1 cup barley

- 1 cup sweet potatoes, peeled and diced

- 1/2 cup carrots, sliced

- 3 cups low-sodium chicken broth

Instructions:

1. Combine diced chicken, barley, diced sweet potatoes, sliced carrots, and chicken broth in the Instant Pot.

2. Set to Manual mode, high pressure, and cook for 12 minutes.

3. Allow a natural release for 10 minutes, then perform a quick release.

4. Stir the banquet thoroughly and let it cool before serving.

Nutritional Information: Per serving - Calories: 280, Protein: 18g, Fat: 6g, Carbohydrates: 30g

Pork and Potato Extravaganza:

Cooking Time: 30 minutes (20 minutes cooking + 10 minutes natural release)

Servings: 6

Ingredients:

- 1 pound lean pork loin, diced

- 1 cup potatoes, peeled and cubed

- 1 cup green beans, chopped

- 1/2 cup apples, peeled and chopped

- 4 cups low-sodium pork broth

Instructions:

1. Sauté diced pork loin until browned in the Instant Pot.

2. Add cubed potatoes, chopped green beans, chopped apples, and pork broth.

3. Set to Manual mode, high pressure, and cook for 20 minutes.

4. Allow a natural release for 10 minutes, then perform a quick release.

5. Stir the extravaganza thoroughly and let it cool before serving.

Nutritional Information: Per serving - Calories: 290, Protein: 18g, Fat: 8g, Carbohydrates: 35g

Lamb and Lentil Luxe:

Cooking Time: 25 minutes (15 minutes cooking + 10 minutes natural release)

Servings: 4

Ingredients:

- 1 cup ground lamb

- 1 cup lentils, rinsed

- 1 cup butternut squash, diced

- 1/2 cup spinach, chopped

- 3 cups low-sodium lamb broth

Instructions:

1. Sauté ground lamb until browned in the Instant Pot.

2. Add rinsed lentils, diced butternut squash, chopped spinach, and lamb broth.

3. Set to Manual mode, high pressure, and cook for 15 minutes.

4. Allow a natural release for 10 minutes, then perform a quick release.

5. Stir the luxe thoroughly and let it cool before serving.

Nutritional Information: Per serving - Calories: 290, Protein: 20g, Fat: 8g, Carbohydrates: 30g

Salmon and Vegetable Bliss:

Cooking Time: 20 minutes (15 minutes cooking + 5 minutes natural release)

Servings: 3

Ingredients:

- 1 cup canned salmon, drained

- 1 cup quinoa, rinsed

- 1 cup zucchini, diced

- 1/2 cup carrots, shredded

- 2 1/2 cups water

Instructions:

1. Combine drained salmon, rinsed quinoa, diced zucchini, shredded carrots, and water in the Instant Pot.

2. Set to Manual mode, high pressure, and cook for 15 minutes.

3. Allow a natural release for 5 minutes, then perform a quick release.

4. Stir the bliss thoroughly and let it cool before serving.

Nutritional Information: Per serving - Calories: 250, Protein: 15g, Fat: 6g, Carbohydrates: 30g

Turkey and Sweet Potato Delicacy:

Cooking Time: 28 minutes (18 minutes cooking + 10 minutes natural release)

Servings: 5

Ingredients:

- 1 pound ground turkey

- 1 cup sweet potatoes, peeled and diced

- 1 cup green beans, cut into small pieces

- 1/2 cup pumpkin puree

- 3 cups low-sodium turkey broth

Instructions:

1. Brown ground turkey in the Instant Pot.

2. Add diced sweet potatoes, cut green beans, pumpkin puree, and turkey broth.

3. Set to Manual mode, high pressure, and cook for 18 minutes.

4. Allow a natural release for 10 minutes, then perform a quick release.

5. Stir the delicacy thoroughly and let it cool before serving.

Nutritional Information: Per serving - Calories: 300, Protein: 18g, Fat: 7g, Carbohydrates: 30g

Chicken and Pumpkin Medley:

Cooking Time: 22 minutes (12 minutes cooking + 10 minutes natural release)

Servings: 4

Ingredients:

- 1 pound boneless, skinless chicken breasts, diced

- 1 cup pumpkin, peeled and diced

- 1/2 cup peas

- 1 cup brown rice

- 3 cups low-sodium chicken broth

Instructions:

1. Add diced chicken, diced pumpkin, peas, brown rice, and chicken broth to the Instant Pot.

2. Set to Manual mode, high pressure, and cook for 12 minutes.

3. Allow a natural release for 10 minutes, then perform a quick release.

4. Stir the medley thoroughly and let it cool before serving.

Nutritional Information: Per serving - Calories: 280, Protein: 18g, Fat: 6g, Carbohydrates: 30g

Pork and Carrot Extravaganza:

Cooking Time: 30 minutes (20 minutes cooking + 10 minutes natural release)

Servings: 6

Ingredients:

- 1 pound lean pork, diced

- 1 cup carrots, sliced

- 1 cup potatoes, peeled and cubed

- 1/2 cup apples, peeled and chopped

- 4 cups low-sodium pork broth

Instructions:

1. Sauté diced pork until browned in the Instant Pot.

2. Add sliced carrots, cubed potatoes, chopped apples, and pork broth.

3. Set to Manual mode, high pressure, and cook for 20 minutes.

4. Allow a natural release for 10 minutes, then perform a quick release.

5. Stir the extravaganza thoroughly and let it cool before serving.

Nutritional Information: Per serving - Calories: 290, Protein: 18g, Fat: 8g, Carbohydrates: 35g

Lamb and Spinach Delight:

Cooking Time: 25 minutes (15 minutes cooking + 10 minutes natural release)

Servings: 4

Ingredients:

- 1 cup ground lamb

- 1 cup spinach, chopped

- 1 cup brown rice

- 1/2 cup peas

- 3 cups low-sodium lamb broth

Instructions:

1. Sauté ground lamb until browned in the Instant Pot.

2. Add chopped spinach, brown rice, peas, and lamb broth.

3. Set to Manual mode, high pressure, and cook for 15 minutes.

4. Allow a natural release for 10 minutes, then perform a quick release.

5. Stir the delight thoroughly and let it cool before serving.

Nutritional Information: Per serving - Calories: 310, Protein: 22g, Fat: 8g, Carbohydrates: 30g

CHAPTER 6
Treats and Snacks

Peanut Butter Pumpkin Bites:

Cooking Time: 10 minutes

Servings: 20 small treats

Ingredients:

- 1 cup canned pumpkin puree
- 1/2 cup peanut butter (unsalted)
- 1 3/4 cups whole wheat flour
- 1/4 cup rolled oats
- 1 egg

Instructions:

1. In a mixing bowl, combine pumpkin puree, peanut butter, whole wheat flour, rolled oats, and the egg.

2. Mix until a dough forms.

3. Roll small portions into bite-sized balls and place them on a baking sheet.

4. Use a fork to flatten each ball slightly.

5. Bake in the Instant Pot using the steam rack for 8 minutes.

6. Allow treats to cool before serving.

Nutritional Information: Per serving - Calories: 60, Protein: 2g, Fat: 3g, Carbohydrates: 7g

Apple Cinnamon Crunchies:

Cooking Time: 12 minutes

Servings: 15 medium-sized treats

Ingredients:

- 2 cups apples, peeled and grated

- 1 1/2 cups oats

- 1/2 cup unsweetened applesauce

- 1/4 cup honey

- 1 teaspoon cinnamon

Instructions:

1. Mix grated apples, oats, applesauce, honey, and cinnamon in a bowl.

2. Scoop spoonfuls of the mixture onto the steam rack in the Instant Pot.

3. Cook on high pressure for 10 minutes.

4. Allow treats to cool and firm up before serving.

Nutritional Information: Per serving - Calories: 70, Protein: 1g, Fat: 1g, Carbohydrates: 16g

Cheesy Sweet Potato Puffs:

Cooking Time: 15 minutes

Servings: 25 small puffs

Ingredients:

- 1 cup sweet potato, cooked and mashed

- 1/2 cup cheddar cheese, shredded

- 1 cup oat flour

- 1 egg

Instructions:

1. In a bowl, combine mashed sweet potato, shredded cheddar cheese, oat flour, and the egg.

2. Mix until a dough forms.

3. Shape small puffs and place them on the steam rack in the Instant Pot.

4. Cook on high pressure for 12 minutes.

5. Allow treats to cool before serving.

Nutritional Information: Per serving - Calories: 40, Protein: 2g, Fat: 2g, Carbohydrates: 5g

Blueberry Banana Biscuits:

Cooking Time: 14 minutes

Servings: 18 biscuits

Ingredients:

- 2 ripe bananas, mashed

- 1/2 cup blueberries, fresh or frozen

- 2 cups oat flour

- 1/4 cup coconut oil, melted

- 1 egg

Instructions:

1. Combine mashed bananas, blueberries, oat flour, melted coconut oil, and the egg in a bowl.

2. Mix until a dough forms.

3. Drop spoonfuls of the dough onto the steam rack in the Instant Pot.

4. Cook on high pressure for 10 minutes.

5. Allow biscuits to cool before serving.

Nutritional Information: Per serving - Calories: 60, Protein: 2g, Fat: 3g, Carbohydrates: 8g

Carrot and Parsley Poppers:

Cooking Time: 12 minutes

Servings: 20 small poppers

Ingredients:

- 1 cup carrots, grated

- 1/2 cup fresh parsley, finely chopped

- 1 1/2 cups brown rice flour

- 1/4 cup chicken broth (low-sodium)

- 1 egg

Instructions:

1. Mix grated carrots, chopped parsley, brown rice flour, chicken broth, and the egg in a bowl.

2. Form small poppers and place them on the steam rack in the Instant Pot.

3. Cook on high pressure for 8 minutes.

4. Allow poppers to cool before serving.

Nutritional Information: Per serving - Calories: 45, Protein: 2g, Fat: 1g, Carbohydrates: 8g

Salmon and Sweet Potato Slices:

Cooking Time: 14 minutes

Servings: 15 slices

Ingredients:

- 1 cup canned salmon, drained

- 1 cup sweet potatoes, peeled and sliced

- 1/2 cup coconut flour

- 1/4 cup plain Greek yogurt

- 1 egg

Instructions:

1. Combine drained salmon, sliced sweet potatoes, coconut flour, Greek yogurt, and the egg in a bowl.

2. Mix until a dough forms.

3. Flatten the dough and cut out small slices or shapes.

4. Place the slices on the steam rack in the Instant Pot.

5. Cook on high pressure for 10 minutes.

6. Allow slices to cool before serving.

Nutritional Information: Per serving - Calories: 55, Protein: 3g, Fat: 2g, Carbohydrates: 6g

Turkey and Cranberry Crunchers:

Cooking Time: 15 minutes

Servings: 20 small crunchers

Ingredients:

- 1 cup ground turkey

- 1/2 cup cranberries, dried

- 1 1/2 cups oat flour

- 1/4 cup pumpkin puree

- 1 egg

Instructions:

1. Brown ground turkey and let it cool.

2. Mix the cooled turkey with dried cranberries, oat flour, pumpkin puree, and the egg in a bowl.

3. Shape small crunchers and place them on the steam rack in the Instant Pot.

4. Cook on high pressure for 12 minutes.

5. Allow crunchers to cool before serving.

Nutritional Information: Per serving - Calories: 50, Protein: 2g, Fat: 2g, Carbohydrates: 7g

Spinach and Chicken Bites:

Cooking Time: 12 minutes

Servings: 25 small bites

Ingredients:

- 1 cup chicken breast, cooked and shredded

- 1/2 cup spinach, finely chopped

- 1 1/2 cups chickpea flour

- 1/4 cup low-sodium chicken broth

- 1 egg

Instructions:

1. In a bowl, combine shredded chicken, chopped spinach, chickpea flour, chicken broth, and the egg.

2. Mix until a dough forms.

3. Shape small bites and place them on the steam rack in the Instant Pot.

4. Cook on high pressure for 8 minutes.

5. Allow bites to cool before serving.

Nutritional Information: Per serving - Calories: 40, Protein: 3g, Fat: 1g, Carbohydrates: 5g

Banana and Blueberry Pupsicles:

Cooking Time: 5 minutes (plus freezing time)

Servings: 6 pupsicles

Ingredients:

- 2 ripe bananas, mashed

- 1/2 cup blueberries, fresh or frozen

- 1 cup plain yogurt (unsweetened)

Instructions:

1. Mix mashed bananas, blueberries, and plain yogurt in a bowl.

2. Pour the mixture into popsicle molds or ice cube trays.

3. Place the molds or trays on the steam rack in the Instant Pot.

4. Cook on high pressure for 2 minutes.

5. Freeze the pupsicles until solid before serving.

Nutritional Information: Per serving - Calories: 70, Protein: 2g, Fat: 2g, Carbohydrates: 12g

Pumpkin and Carrot Muffins:

Cooking Time: 15 minutes

Servings: 12 muffins

Ingredients:

- 1 cup canned pumpkin puree

- 1/2 cup carrots, grated

- 1 1/2 cups whole wheat flour

- 1/4 cup coconut oil, melted

- 1 egg

Instructions:

1. Combine pumpkin puree, grated carrots, whole wheat flour, melted coconut oil, and the egg in a bowl.

2. Mix until a batter forms.

3. Spoon the batter into muffin cups and place them on the steam rack in the Instant Pot.

4. Cook on high pressure for 10 minutes.

5. Allow muffins to cool before serving.

Nutritional Information: Per serving - Calories: 85, Protein: 2g, Fat: 4g, Carbohydrates: 11g

CHAPTER 7

Special Diets for Dogs with Dietary Restrictions

Grain-Free Turkey and Vegetable Stew:

Cooking Time: 25 minutes (15 minutes cooking + 10 minutes natural release)

Servings: 4

Ingredients:

- 1 pound ground turkey
- 1 cup zucchini, diced
- 1 cup pumpkin, peeled and cubed
- 1/2 cup carrots, sliced
- 3 cups bone broth (no onions or garlic)

Instructions:

1. Brown ground turkey in the Instant Pot.
2. Add diced zucchini, cubed pumpkin, sliced carrots, and bone broth.
3. Set to Manual mode, high pressure, and cook for 15 minutes.
4. Allow a natural release for 10 minutes, then perform a quick release.
5. Stir the stew thoroughly and let it cool before serving.

Nutritional Information: Per serving - Calories: 280, Protein: 18g, Fat: 6g, Carbohydrates: 30g

Sensitive Stomach Chicken and Rice Porridge:

Cooking Time: 20 minutes (15 minutes cooking + 5 minutes natural release)

Servings: 3

Ingredients:

- 1 cup shredded chicken breast

- 1 cup white rice, cooked

- 1 cup carrots, finely grated

- 2 cups low-sodium chicken broth

Instructions:

1. Combine shredded chicken, cooked white rice, grated carrots, and chicken broth in the Instant Pot.

2. Set to Manual mode, high pressure, and cook for 15 minutes.

3. Allow a natural release for 5 minutes, then perform a quick release.

4. Stir the porridge thoroughly and let it cool before serving.

Nutritional Information: Per serving - Calories: 250, Protein: 15g, Fat: 5g, Carbohydrates: 30g

Limited Ingredient Lamb and Potato Casserole:

Cooking Time: 28 minutes (18 minutes cooking + 10 minutes natural release)

Servings: 5

Ingredients:

- 1 cup ground lamb

- 1 cup potatoes, peeled and diced

- 1 cup green beans, cut into small pieces

- 3 cups low-sodium lamb broth

Instructions:

1. Brown ground lamb in the Instant Pot.

2. Add diced potatoes, cut green beans, and lamb broth.

3. Set to Manual mode, high pressure, and cook for 18 minutes.

4. Allow a natural release for 10 minutes, then perform a quick release.

5. Stir the casserole thoroughly and let it cool before serving.

Nutritional Information: Per serving - Calories: 320, Protein: 20g, Fat: 8g, Carbohydrates: 35g

Hypoallergenic Salmon and Quinoa Medley:

Cooking Time: 25 minutes (15 minutes cooking + 10 minutes natural release)

Servings: 4

Ingredients:

- 1 cup canned salmon, drained

- 1 cup quinoa, rinsed

- 1 cup sweet potatoes, diced

- 3 cups low-sodium fish broth

Instructions:

1. Combine drained salmon, rinsed quinoa, diced sweet potatoes, and fish broth in the Instant Pot.

2. Set to Manual mode, high pressure, and cook for 15 minutes.

3. Allow a natural release for 10 minutes, then perform a quick release.

4. Stir the medley thoroughly and let it cool before serving.

Nutritional Information: Per serving - Calories: 250, Protein: 16g, Fat: 6g, Carbohydrates: 30g

Low-Fat Turkey and Vegetable Stir-Fry:

Cooking Time: 22 minutes (12 minutes cooking + 10 minutes natural release)

Servings: 4

Ingredients:

- 1 pound ground turkey breast

- 1 cup broccoli, chopped

- 1 cup carrots, julienned

- 1/2 cup green beans, sliced

- 3 cups low-sodium turkey broth

Instructions:

1. Brown ground turkey breast in the Instant Pot.

2. Add chopped broccoli, julienned carrots, sliced green beans, and turkey broth.

3. Set to Manual mode, high pressure, and cook for 12 minutes.

4. Allow a natural release for 10 minutes, then perform a quick release.

5. Stir the stir-fry thoroughly and let it cool before serving.

Nutritional Information: Per serving - Calories: 280, Protein: 18g, Fat: 5g, Carbohydrates: 30g

Weight Management Chicken and Pea Casserole:

Cooking Time: 30 minutes (20 minutes cooking + 10 minutes natural release)

Servings: 6

Ingredients:

- 1 pound boneless, skinless chicken breasts, diced

- 1 cup peas

- 1 cup sweet potatoes, peeled and cubed

- 4 cups low-sodium chicken broth

Instructions:

1. Add diced chicken, peas, cubed sweet potatoes, and chicken broth to the Instant Pot.

2. Set to Manual mode, high pressure, and cook for 20 minutes.

3. Allow a natural release for 10 minutes, then perform a quick release.

4. Stir the casserole thoroughly and let it cool before serving.

Nutritional Information: Per serving - Calories: 290, Protein: 18g, Fat: 5g, Carbohydrates: 35g

Digestive Health Beef and Pumpkin Stew:

Cooking Time: 25 minutes (15 minutes cooking + 10 minutes natural release)

Servings: 4

Ingredients:

- 1 pound lean beef stew meat, diced

- 1 cup pumpkin puree

- 1 cup brown rice, cooked

- 3 cups low-sodium beef broth

Instructions:

1. Sauté diced beef in the Instant Pot until browned.

2. Add pumpkin puree, cooked brown rice, and beef broth.

3. Set to Manual mode, high pressure, and cook for 15 minutes.

4. Allow a natural release for 10 minutes, then perform a quick release.

5. Stir the stew thoroughly and let it cool before serving.

Nutritional Information: Per serving - Calories: 320, Protein: 20g, Fat: 8g, Carbohydrates: 35g

Renal Support Chicken and Rice Pilaf:

Cooking Time: 28 minutes (18 minutes cooking + 10 minutes natural release)

Servings: 5

Ingredients:

- 1 pound chicken thighs, boneless and skinless, diced

- 1 cup white rice, cooked

- 1 cup carrots, sliced

- 3 cups low-sodium chicken broth

Instructions:

1. Brown diced chicken thighs in the Instant Pot.

2. Add cooked white rice, sliced carrots, and chicken broth.

3. Set to Manual mode, high pressure, and cook for 18 minutes.

4. Allow a natural release for 10 minutes, then perform a quick release.

5. Stir the pilaf thoroughly and let it cool before serving.

Nutritional Information: Per serving - Calories: 300, Protein: 18g, Fat: 7g, Carbohydrates: 30g

Senior Dog Turkey and Barley Stew:

Cooking Time: 22 minutes (12 minutes cooking + 10 minutes natural release)

Servings: 4

Ingredients:

- 1 pound ground turkey

- 1 cup barley

- 1 cup sweet potatoes, peeled and diced

- 3 cups low-sodium turkey broth

Instructions:

1. Brown ground turkey in the Instant Pot.

2. Add barley, diced sweet potatoes, and turkey broth.

3. Set to Manual mode, high pressure, and cook for 12 minutes.

4. Allow a natural release for 10 minutes, then perform a quick release.

5. Stir the stew thoroughly and let it cool before serving.

Nutritional Information: Per serving - Calories: 280, Protein: 18g, Fat: 6g, Carbohydrates: 30g

Joint Health Fish and Vegetable Mash:

Cooking Time: 25 minutes (15 minutes cooking + 10 minutes natural release)

Servings: 4

Ingredients:

- 1 cup whitefish fillets, diced

- 1 cup sweet potatoes, peeled and cubed

- 1 cup green peas

- 3 cups low-sodium fish broth

Instructions:

1. Combine diced whitefish, cubed sweet potatoes, green peas, and fish broth in the Instant Pot.

2. Set to Manual mode, high pressure, and cook for 15 minutes.

3. Allow a natural release for 10 minutes, then perform a quick release.

4. Mash the mixture thoroughly and let it cool before serving.

Nutritional Information: Per serving - Calories: 260, Protein: 16g, Fat: 5g, Carbohydrates: 30g

CONCLUSION

As we conclude this culinary odyssey through the pages of the Instant Pot Dog Food Cookbook, I am filled with a profound sense of gratitude for the shared moments and the unspoken connections that bind us to our loyal companions. The journey from my childhood love for Dan to the creation of this cookbook has been a tapestry woven with threads of love, learning, and healing.

Each recipe within these pages is a testament to the transformative power of mindful nutrition. It echoes the laughter that reverberates through our homes, the pawprints that grace our hearts, and the unwavering loyalty that defines the canine-human connection. As you embark on this culinary adventure, may every meal become a symphony of health and happiness for your cherished pets.

But this journey doesn't end here. I invite you to bring your own stories into this narrative, to share the experiences of joy, healing, and newfound vitality that these recipes bring to your dogs. Your feedback is the heartbeat of this cookbook, a melody that continues to evolve with each wag of a tail, each eager lick, and each satisfied sigh.

Feedback: Your Voice in Our Culinary Symphony

Your thoughts, experiences, and insights are invaluable. If a particular recipe became a cherished favorite in your household, or if you discovered unexpected moments of connection through the act of preparing a meal for your furry friend, share those tales with us. Your feedback is the bridge that connects the heart of this cookbook with the beating hearts of dogs around the world.

Were there challenges you faced, or perhaps culinary triumphs that surprised even the most discerning canine palate? I encourage you to join our community, a gathering of dog lovers dedicated to elevating the well-being of our pets through mindful nutrition. Your stories inspire us, fueling our commitment to continually refine and expand the offerings within these culinary pages.

Together, let us celebrate the boundless joy that dogs bring into our lives. Let us share the triumphs and tribulations of this culinary journey. Your feedback is not just welcomed; it is cherished, for it transforms this cookbook into a living, breathing testament to the love we share with our furry companions.

As we part ways for now, know that this cookbook is not just a collection of recipes; it is an extension of our shared journey. May every meal you prepare be a gesture of love, a salute to health, and a celebration of the extraordinary bond we share with our dogs.

Thank you for joining me on this adventure, and I eagerly await the symphony of your feedback, each note a melody in the culinary ode to canine wellness.

BONUS 1

Effective Dog Training Tips for a Happy and Obedient Companion

Training your dog is a rewarding journey that fosters a strong bond between you and your furry friend. In this chapter, we will explore essential dog training tips to help you build a well-behaved and happy companion.

1. Start Early and Be Consistent

Begin training your dog as early as possible. Puppies are like sponges, absorbing information and adapting quickly. Establish a consistent routine for training sessions to reinforce positive behavior.

2. Use Positive Reinforcement

Positive reinforcement is a powerful tool in dog training. Reward your dog with treats, praise, or play when they exhibit the desired behavior. This creates a positive association and motivates them to repeat the behavior.

3. Short and Engaging Sessions

Keep training sessions short and engaging, especially for younger dogs. Aim for 5-10 minutes of focused training to maintain your dog's interest and prevent boredom.

4. Be Patient and Stay Calm

Patience is key. Dogs respond better to calm and patient trainers. If your dog makes a mistake, avoid punishment; instead, redirect them to the correct behavior and reward when they get it right.

5. Use Clear and Consistent Commands

Dogs thrive on consistency and clarity. Use clear, simple commands for each behavior you want to teach. Consistency in your commands and expectations helps your dog understand what is expected of them.

6. Socialization is Crucial

Expose your dog to various environments, people, and other animals from a young age. Proper socialization helps prevent behavioral issues and ensures your dog is comfortable in different situations.

7. Master Basic Commands

Teach essential commands like sit, stay, come, and leave it. These commands form the foundation for a well-behaved dog and are essential for their safety and the safety of others.

8. Use Leash Training Techniques

Leash training is vital for both your dog's safety and the enjoyment of walks. Teach your dog to walk politely on a leash, avoiding pulling or lunging.

9. Address Undesirable Behaviors Early

If you notice undesirable behaviors like excessive barking or chewing, address them promptly. Identify the root cause, redirect their attention, and provide alternatives to discourage negative habits.

10. Consider Professional Training Classes

Enroll in a dog training class or seek the help of a professional trainer if you encounter challenges. Professional guidance can provide valuable insights and techniques to overcome specific issues.

11. Integrate Training into Daily Life

Incorporate training into your daily routine. Use mealtime, walks, and play sessions as opportunities to reinforce good behavior and practice commands.

12. Regular Exercise and Mental Stimulation

Ensure your dog receives regular exercise and mental stimulation. A tired dog is a well-behaved dog. Engaging activities like puzzle toys, agility exercises, and interactive play keep their minds sharp and reduce boredom.

13. Monitor Health and Well-being

Behavioral changes can sometimes be indicators of underlying health issues. If your dog's behavior shifts suddenly, consult with your veterinarian to rule out any medical concerns.

BONUS 2
30 DAY MEAL PLAN

WEEK 1

Day 1:

- **Breakfast:** Salmon and Sweet Potato Slices

- **Lunch:** Turkey and Cranberry Crunchers (snack-sized)

- **Dinner:** Chicken and Pumpkin Medley

- **Snack:** Apple Cinnamon Crunchies

Day 2:

- **Breakfast:** Cheesy Sweet Potato Puffs

- **Lunch:** Turkey and Sweet Potato Delicacy

- **Dinner:** Salmon and Vegetable Bliss

- **Snack:** Blueberry Banana Biscuits

Day 3:

- **Breakfast:** Chicken and Pumpkin Medley

- **Lunch:** Spinach and Chicken Bites

- **Dinner:** Pork and Carrot Extravaganza

- **Snack:** Carrot and Parsley Poppers

Day 4:

- **Breakfast:** Blueberry Banana Biscuits

- **Lunch:** Cheesy Sweet Potato Puffs

- **Dinner:** Chicken and Pumpkin Medley

- **Snack:** Peanut Butter Pumpkin Bites

Day 5:

- **Breakfast:** Carrot and Parsley Poppers

- **Lunch:** Salmon and Vegetable Bliss

- **Dinner:** Turkey and Cranberry Crunchers (snack-sized)

- **Snack:** Banana and Blueberry Pupsicles

Day 6:

- **Breakfast:** Spinach and Chicken Bites

- **Lunch:** Apple Cinnamon Crunchies

- **Dinner:** Pork and Carrot Extravaganza

- **Snack:** Cheesy Sweet Potato Puffs

Day 7:

- **Breakfast:** Banana and Blueberry Pupsicles

- **Lunch:** Blueberry Banana Biscuits

- **Dinner:** Chicken and Pumpkin Medley

- **Snack:** Turkey and Sweet Potato Delicacy

WEEK 2

Day 8:

- **Breakfast:** Turkey and Sweet Potato Delicacy

- **Lunch:** Peanut Butter Pumpkin Bites

- **Dinner:** Spinach and Chicken Bites

- **Snack:** Apple Cinnamon Crunchies

Day 9:

- **Breakfast:** Pork and Carrot Extravaganza

- **Lunch:** Blueberry Banana Biscuits

- **Dinner:** Salmon and Vegetable Bliss

- **Snack:** Turkey and Cranberry Crunchers (snack-sized)

Day 10:

- **Breakfast:** Cheesy Sweet Potato Puffs

- **Lunch:** Banana and Blueberry Pupsicles

- **Dinner:** Chicken and Pumpkin Medley

- **Snack:** Carrot and Parsley Poppers

Day 11:

- **Breakfast:** Chicken and Pumpkin Medley

- **Lunch:** Cheesy Sweet Potato Puffs

- **Dinner:** Pork and Carrot Extravaganza

- **Snack:** Spinach and Chicken Bites

Day 12:

- **Breakfast:** Salmon and Sweet Potato Slices

- **Lunch:** Turkey and Cranberry Crunchers (snack-sized)

- **Dinner:** Chicken and Pumpkin Medley

- **Snack:** Apple Cinnamon Crunchies

Day 13:

- **Breakfast:** Blueberry Banana Biscuits

- **Lunch:** Cheesy Sweet Potato Puffs

- **Dinner:** Turkey and Sweet Potato Delicacy

- **Snack:** Peanut Butter Pumpkin Bites

Day 14:

- **Breakfast:** Carrot and Parsley Poppers

- **Lunch:** Banana and Blueberry Pupsicles

- **Dinner:** Pork and Carrot Extravaganza

- **Snack:** Blueberry Banana Biscuits

WEEK 3

Day 15:

- **Breakfast:** Spinach and Chicken Bites

- **Lunch:** Apple Cinnamon Crunchies

- **Dinner:** Turkey and Cranberry Crunchers (snack-sized)

- **Snack:** Cheesy Sweet Potato Puffs

Day 16:

- **Breakfast:** Banana and Blueberry Pupsicles

- **Lunch:** Blueberry Banana Biscuits

- **Dinner:** Chicken and Pumpkin Medley

- **Snack:** Turkey and Sweet Potato Delicacy

Day 17:

- **Breakfast:** Turkey and Sweet Potato Delicacy

- **Lunch:** Peanut Butter Pumpkin Bites

- **Dinner:** Spinach and Chicken Bites

- **Snack:** Apple Cinnamon Crunchies

Day 18:

- **Breakfast:** Pork and Carrot Extravaganza

- **Lunch:** Blueberry Banana Biscuits

- **Dinner:** Salmon and Vegetable Bliss

- **Snack:** Turkey and Cranberry Crunchers (snack-sized)

Day 19:

- **Breakfast:** Cheesy Sweet Potato Puffs

- **Lunch:** Banana and Blueberry Pupsicles

- **Dinner:** Chicken and Pumpkin Medley

- **Snack:** Carrot and Parsley Poppers

Day 20:

- **Breakfast:** Salmon and Sweet Potato Slices

- **Lunch:** Turkey and Cranberry Crunchers (snack-sized)

- **Dinner:** Pork and Carrot Extravaganza

- **Snack:** Spinach and Chicken Bites

Day 21:

- **Breakfast:** Chicken and Pumpkin Medley

- **Lunch:** Cheesy Sweet Potato Puffs

- **Dinner:** Pork and Carrot Extravaganza

- **Snack:** Spinach and Chicken Bites

WEEK 4

Day 22:

- **Breakfast:** Salmon and Sweet Potato Slices

- **Lunch:** Turkey and Cranberry Crunchers (snack-sized)

- **Dinner:** Chicken and Pumpkin Medley

- **Snack:** Apple Cinnamon Crunchies

Day 23:

- **Breakfast:** Blueberry Banana Biscuits

- **Lunch:** Cheesy Sweet Potato Puffs

- **Dinner:** Turkey and Sweet Potato Delicacy

- **Snack:** Peanut Butter Pumpkin Bites

Day 24:

- **Breakfast:** Carrot and Parsley Poppers

- **Lunch:** Banana and Blueberry Pupsicles

- **Dinner:** Pork and Carrot Extravaganza

- **Snack:** Blueberry Banana Biscuits

Day 25:

- **Breakfast:** Spinach and Chicken Bites

- **Lunch:** Apple Cinnamon Crunchies

- **Dinner:** Turkey and Cranberry Crunchers (snack-sized)

- **Snack:** Cheesy Sweet Potato Puffs

Day 26:

- **Breakfast:** Banana and Blueberry Pupsicles

- **Lunch:** Blueberry Banana Biscuits

- **Dinner:** Chicken and Pumpkin Medley

- **Snack:** Turkey and Sweet Potato Delicacy

Day 27:

- **Breakfast:** Turkey and Sweet Potato Delicacy

- **Lunch:** Peanut Butter Pumpkin Bites

- **Dinner:** Spinach and Chicken Bites

- **Snack:** Apple Cinnamon Crunchies

Day 28:

- **Breakfast:** Pork and Carrot Extravaganza

- **Lunch:** Blueberry Banana Biscuits

- **Dinner:** Salmon and Vegetable Bliss

- **Snack:** Turkey and Cranberry Crunchers (snack-sized)

Day 29:

- **Breakfast:** Cheesy Sweet Potato Puffs

- **Lunch:** Banana and Blueberry Pupsicles

- **Dinner:** Chicken and Pumpkin Medley

- **Snack:** Carrot and Parsley Poppers

Day 30:

- **Breakfast:** Salmon and Sweet Potato Slices

- **Lunch:** Turkey and Cranberry Crunchers (snack-sized)

- **Dinner:** Pork and Carrot Extravaganza

- **Snack:** Spinach and Chicken Bites

MEAL PLANNER JOURNAL

WEEKLY —

Meal Planner

Week of: _____

Monday		Tuesday		Wednesday
BREAKFAST		BREAKFAST		BREAKFAST
LUNCH		LUNCH		LUNCH
DINNER		DINNER		DINNER
SNACK		SNACK		SNACK

Thursday		Friday		Saturday
BREAKFAST		BREAKFAST		BREAKFAST
LUNCH		LUNCH		LUNCH
DINNER		DINNER		DINNER
SNACK		SNACK		SNACK

Sunday	NOTES:
BREAKFAST	
LUNCH	
DINNER	
SNACK	

Meal Planner

Week of: _____

Monday		Tuesday		Wednesday	
BREAKFAST		BREAKFAST		BREAKFAST	
LUNCH		LUNCH		LUNCH	
DINNER		DINNER		DINNER	
SNACK		SNACK		SNACK	

Thursday		Friday		Saturday	
BREAKFAST		BREAKFAST		BREAKFAST	
LUNCH		LUNCH		LUNCH	
DINNER		DINNER		DINNER	
SNACK		SNACK		SNACK	

Sunday		NOTES:
BREAKFAST		
LUNCH		
DINNER		
SNACK		

Meal Planner

Week of:

Monday	Tuesday	Wednesday
BREAKFAST	BREAKFAST	BREAKFAST
LUNCH	LUNCH	LUNCH
DINNER	DINNER	DINNER
SNACK	SNACK	SNACK

Thursday	Friday	Saturday
BREAKFAST	BREAKFAST	BREAKFAST
LUNCH	LUNCH	LUNCH
DINNER	DINNER	DINNER
SNACK	SNACK	SNACK

Sunday	NOTES:
BREAKFAST	
LUNCH	
DINNER	
SNACK	

WEEKLY —

Meal Planner

Week of:
_____

Monday	Tuesday	Wednesday
BREAKFAST	BREAKFAST	BREAKFAST
LUNCH	LUNCH	LUNCH
DINNER	DINNER	DINNER
SNACK	SNACK	SNACK

Thursday	Friday	Saturday
BREAKFAST	BREAKFAST	BREAKFAST
LUNCH	LUNCH	LUNCH
DINNER	DINNER	DINNER
SNACK	SNACK	SNACK

Sunday	NOTES:
BREAKFAST	
LUNCH	
DINNER	
SNACK	

Meal Planner

Week of:

Monday	Tuesday	Wednesday
BREAKFAST	BREAKFAST	BREAKFAST
LUNCH	LUNCH	LUNCH
DINNER	DINNER	DINNER
SNACK	SNACK	SNACK

Thursday	Friday	Saturday
BREAKFAST	BREAKFAST	BREAKFAST
LUNCH	LUNCH	LUNCH
DINNER	DINNER	DINNER
SNACK	SNACK	SNACK

Sunday	NOTES:
BREAKFAST	
LUNCH	
DINNER	
SNACK	

WEEKLY —

Meal Planner

Week of:

Monday	Tuesday	Wednesday
BREAKFAST	BREAKFAST	BREAKFAST
LUNCH	LUNCH	LUNCH
DINNER	DINNER	DINNER
SNACK	SNACK	SNACK

Thursday	Friday	Saturday
BREAKFAST	BREAKFAST	BREAKFAST
LUNCH	LUNCH	LUNCH
DINNER	DINNER	DINNER
SNACK	SNACK	SNACK

Sunday	NOTES:
BREAKFAST	
LUNCH	
DINNER	
SNACK	

WEEKLY —

Meal Planner

Week of: _____

Monday

BREAKFAST
_____

LUNCH
_____

DINNER
_____

SNACK
_____

Tuesday

BREAKFAST
_____

LUNCH
_____

DINNER
_____

SNACK
_____

Wednesday

BREAKFAST
_____

LUNCH
_____

DINNER
_____

SNACK
_____

Thursday

BREAKFAST
_____

LUNCH
_____

DINNER
_____

SNACK
_____

Friday

BREAKFAST
_____

LUNCH
_____

DINNER
_____

SNACK
_____

Saturday

BREAKFAST
_____

LUNCH
_____

DINNER
_____

SNACK
_____

Sunday

BREAKFAST
_____

LUNCH
_____

DINNER
_____

SNACK
_____

NOTES:
_____

WEEKLY —

Meal Planner

Week of: _____

Monday	Tuesday	Wednesday
BREAKFAST	BREAKFAST	BREAKFAST
LUNCH	LUNCH	LUNCH
DINNER	DINNER	DINNER
SNACK	SNACK	SNACK

Thursday	Friday	Saturday
BREAKFAST	BREAKFAST	BREAKFAST
LUNCH	LUNCH	LUNCH
DINNER	DINNER	DINNER
SNACK	SNACK	SNACK

Sunday	NOTES:
BREAKFAST	
LUNCH	
DINNER	
SNACK	

Meal Planner

Week of:

Monday	Tuesday	Wednesday
BREAKFAST	BREAKFAST	BREAKFAST
LUNCH	LUNCH	LUNCH
DINNER	DINNER	DINNER
SNACK	SNACK	SNACK

Thursday	Friday	Saturday
BREAKFAST	BREAKFAST	BREAKFAST
LUNCH	LUNCH	LUNCH
DINNER	DINNER	DINNER
SNACK	SNACK	SNACK

Sunday	NOTES:
BREAKFAST	
LUNCH	
DINNER	
SNACK	

WEEKLY —

Meal Planner

Week of: _____

Monday	Tuesday	Wednesday
BREAKFAST	BREAKFAST	BREAKFAST
LUNCH	LUNCH	LUNCH
DINNER	DINNER	DINNER
SNACK	SNACK	SNACK

Thursday	Friday	Saturday
BREAKFAST	BREAKFAST	BREAKFAST
LUNCH	LUNCH	LUNCH
DINNER	DINNER	DINNER
SNACK	SNACK	SNACK

Sunday	NOTES:
BREAKFAST	
LUNCH	
DINNER	
SNACK	

MONTHLY —

Meal Planner

Month of: _____

Sun	Mon	Tues	Wed	Thurs	Fri	Sai